Super Structures
International Space Station

by Julie Murray

Dash!
LEVELED READERS
An Imprint of Abdo Zoom • abdopublishing.com

3

Dash!
LEVELED READERS

Level 1 – Beginning
Short and simple sentences with familiar words or patterns for children who are beginning to understand how letters and sounds go together.

Level 2 – Emerging
Longer words and sentences with more complex language patterns for readers who are practicing common words and letter sounds.

Level 3 – Transitional
More developed language and vocabulary for readers who are becoming more independent.

abdopublishing.com

Published by Abdo Zoom, a division of ABDO, PO Box 398166, Minneapolis, Minnesota 55439.
Copyright © 2019 by Abdo Consulting Group, Inc. International copyrights reserved in all countries.
No part of this book may be reproduced in any form without written permission from the publisher.
Dash!™ is a trademark and logo of Abdo Zoom.

Printed in the United States of America, North Mankato, Minnesota.
052018
092018

Photo Credits: iStock, NASA, NASA/ESA, Shutterstock
Production Contributors: Kenny Abdo, Jennie Forsberg, Grace Hansen, John Hansen
Design Contributors: Dorothy Toth, Neil Klinepier

Library of Congress Control Number: 2017960594

Publisher's Cataloging in Publication Data

Names: Murray, Julie, author.
Title: International Space Station / by Julie Murray.
Description: Minneapolis, Minnesota : Abdo Zoom, 2019. | Series: Super structures |
    Includes online resources and index.
Identifiers: ISBN 9781532123115 (lib.bdg.) | ISBN 9781532124099 (ebook) |
    ISBN 9781532124587 (Read-to-me ebook)
Subjects: LCSH: Space stations--Juvenile literature. | Aerospace engineering--Juvenile literature. |
    Large space structures (Astronautics)--Juvenile literature. | Architecture--building design--Juvenile
    literature.
Classification: DDC 629.442--dc23

Table of Contents

International Space Station

The International Space Station (ISS) is a special place. Astronauts from different countries live and work there. Six people can live on the ISS at a time. Most stay for about six months.

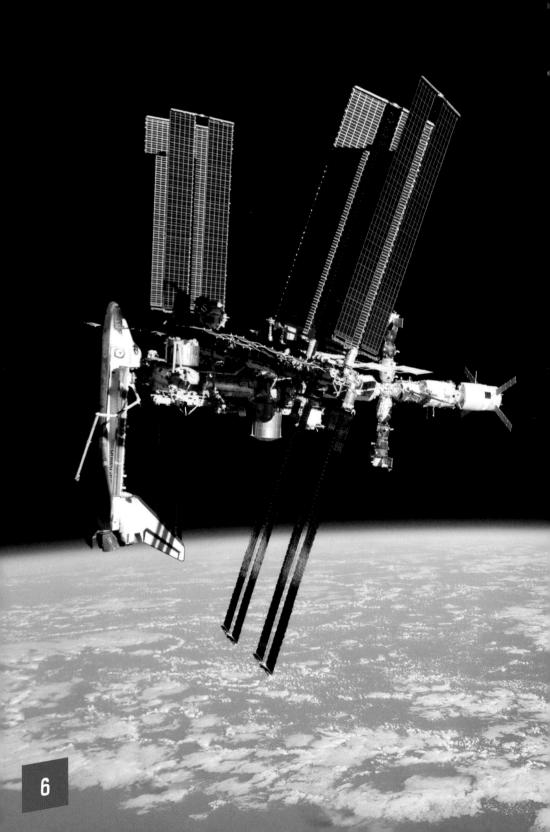

The ISS flies 220 miles (354 km) above Earth. It travels 17,500 mph (28,163 kph). It only takes 90 minutes to **orbit** one time around Earth!

Building the ISS

Sixteen nations worked together to build the ISS. It has more than 100 different sections! They were built on Earth.

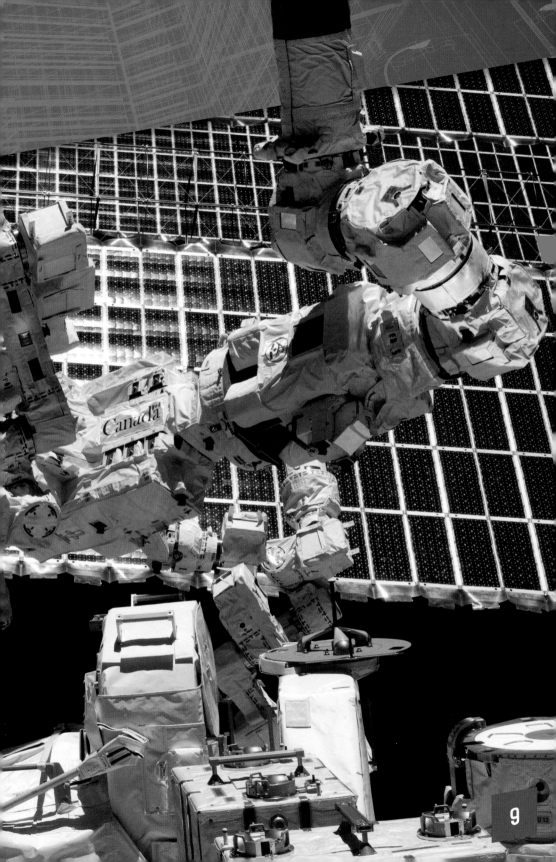

American and Russian space craft brought the sections to the ISS. It took 40 space missions to put it together. The ISS is bigger than a football field!

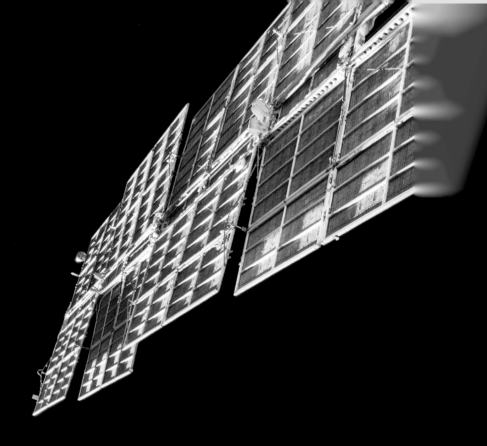

The first piece was called the Zarya module. It went up in November 1998 on a Russian Proton rocket. The first crew started living on the ISS on November 2, 2000.

The outer layer of the ISS is made of aluminum. There are layers of **Kevlar** and **ceramic fibers** too. There are solar arrays on each side of the ISS. These absorb energy from the sun and provide electrical power to the space station.

Scott Kelly, a US astronaut, lived on the ISS for 240 days. He went on three **spacewalks** and conducted many different experiments. He returned to Earth in March 2016.

17

Life on the ISS

Life on the ISS is not easy. There is no **gravity** in space. Human muscles weaken because they are not used as much. Astronauts must be strong and healthy. They exercise in space.

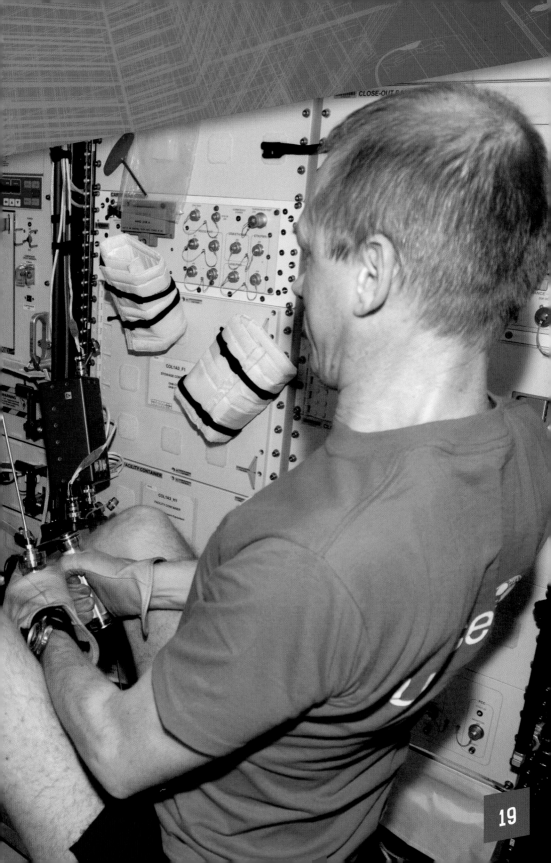

The astronauts also have to do **spacewalks**. They wear special suits to protect them. They are attached to long cables so they don't float away!

More Facts

- Construction of the ISS was completed in 2011. It took 13 years and cost more than $100 billion to build.

- The ISS weighs almost one million pounds (453,592 kg). That is equal to the weight of 320 cars!

- The ISS travels around Earth once every 90 minutes. Astronauts get to enjoy 16 sunrises and sunsets every day!

Glossary

ceramic fiber – one of several types of synthetic mineral wool that is resistant to temperatures above 1,830 degrees F (1,000 degrees C).

gravity – a force of attraction that exists between any two masses, any two bodies, or any two particles.

Kevlar – a high-strength material.

orbit – to travel around something in a curved path.

spacewalk – an activity by an astronaut in space outside a spacecraft.

Index

Online Resources

Booklinks
NONFICTION NETWORK
FREE! ONLINE NONFICTION RESOURCES

To learn more about the International Space Station, please visit **abdobooklinks.com**. These links are routinely monitored and updated to provide the most current information available.